# Blooming Petals

A JOURNEY OF SELF LOVE

Anwesha Das

# Preface

The reader here is presented with a tale of self-love. The majority writing of this book consists of poetry, quotes and prose. The first two contents inspire healing from traumatic experiences in life and the last two contents reflect on self-discovery and the magnificent power of self-love.

Love has a magic that can mend a broken heart. We often look for that magic in someone else when we ourselves carry the source of magic inside us. That source of magic is called self-love.

The journey of self-love is not an easy one. The roads may be bumpy and full of self-doubts that block us from reaching our destination and discovering all the greatness we have within ourselves. We often get distracted and we depend on another person to love ourselves but in most cases, we end up with disappointments and pain. But we can heal from that pain with self-love.

Note—Self-love is not selfish, self-loving is self-awakening.



Instagram @_poetry.and.nature

# Table of Contents

Wilted like the petals

We often end up giving ourselves away to those who we should keep away from.

*~ that's how we meet disappointments.*

# Blooming Petals

You have risked it all,

You walked through lightning and thunder

Just to get wet once in the rain of love.


~ *Was it worth it?*

Love is supposed to make you feel alive,

Love isn't supposed to drain the life out of you.

Blooming Petals

I see you giving away all your love to someone who doesn't know what love is. You have a kind heart. You believe your love will heal them. You patiently nourish them in the hope that they will love you back someday.

But most of the broken people don't heal no matter how much love you pour into them because they're in denial with themselves. They think they're fine. You cannot heal someone who thinks they're fine. Unfortunately you cannot change their mindset. All you can do is watch and learn.

Know what you're doing. Set boundaries. Love them but don't forget to love yourself. Don't lose yourself in the process of healing others when they don't even appreciate you.

Over-watering buds won't make them bloom faster.

# Blooming Petals

Giving efforts to wrong places

Leave you wilted

While giving efforts to right places

Make you bloom.

All the times you've wasted on people

Who took you for granted,

I wish you would've invested in yourself.

The way you took care of them,

I wish you'd have taken care of yourself.

It's never too late to see people

For who they really are.

It's never too late to start loving yourself.

Nourish yourself.

Grow beautifully.

Blooming Petals

True love can do magic and wonder

But don't lose your way wandering in wrong places.

Don't burn yourself to provide light like the sun

For people who only take but give none.

Toxic people bring out the worst in you. Who were you before you met them? Who have you become when you're around them? Do you want to be the person you're becoming? If the answer is no, step out. Don't lower your standards to be at the same level as them. You're better than that.

The best way to respond to disrespect is moving on. Don't respond to disrespect with disrespect because you're not that person. Don't respond to disrespect with silence because they will take disadvantage of your silence. The best thing you can do is walk away and never look back. Restore your peace of mind. Surround yourself with people who bring out the best in you. You need to choose a safe environment for yourself in order to grow.

Planting flowers attracts butterflies

While dirty rooms attract cobwebs,

Choose who you spend your time with carefully.

# Blooming Petals

When you choose to see the good in you,

The universe will send the good vibes to you.

Loving someone who is boiling with rage

Is like jumping to a volcano with a glass of water.


~ *anger issues and disrespect*

# Blooming Petals

People who lack respect for you

Look down upon the person who you are.

Why do you want to be around people

Who do not accept your true self?

Being treated with disrespect for too long makes you lose your self confidence. When you look at the mirror, all you can see is a figure with emptiness. The shine is gone. Self-esteem is gone. You end up with a mind full of self doubts. You don't see your value anymore. You allow them to treat you poorly day by day cause you believe you deserve no better.

But self doubts are passing clouds. They come and go. You are the eternal sunshine. Only you have the ability to shine bright and make those dark clouds disappear. It's never too late to remove yourself from toxic people who kill your self esteem.

Give yourself some time to heal. Hold onto positivity. You'll reach your confident form once again.

# Blooming Petals

Break free from a grip that suffocates you.

Don't let them manipulate you into believing you are a rhinestone when actually you're a diamond.

~ *know your worth*

# Blooming Petals

Sad memories are a bird feather,

Shed them and fly free.

Embrace the good in life.

New habits will start to form

When you get rid of the old ones.

Good people will come into your life

When you finally remove the toxic ones.

# Blooming Petals

Form yourself slowly, beautifully and powerfully.

Breaking is okay

But don't ever give up on the idea

That you can repair.

# Blooming Petals

A little warmth

And a little bit of care

Revive the wilted petals.

Water your roots with self love

And bloom freshly.

When you heal,

Scars don't make you feel insecure,

They inspire you.

Cut negativity like the weeds

You sit by the beach,

You watch the waves break.

They break countless times

But still they come back stronger.

That's power.

# Blooming Petals

Some people are like parasites,

Don't be their host.

Don't let them use you

And destroy you.

Take back your strength.

Your life is a garden,

Your soul is a flower.

Many weed will grow

But it's your responsibility

To cut them off of your garden

So that you can bloom graciously.

Negativity is the enemy of growth. A negative mind always tells how you *cannot.* The fears leave you stuck in one place and pause your growth.

Find against your own mind when it's necessary.

Do you remember the fog in winter?

When you look ahead,

Everything seems blurry.

When you keep on walking,

The view gets clearer with each step.

Our minds are the same.

Self doubts fog our confidence

And block us from seeing the good in us

But with each step of introspection,

We find our way back to a clearer perspective.

# Blooming Petals

Anxiety oversteps

But you have the power to outspeed it.

When you've always been told that you don't have what it takes to reach your goals, your subconscious mind believes it. The doubts crawl to your conscious mind and make you doubt yourself. You are climbing the stairway of insecurities and you're only going down. This happens to the very best of us.

The only way to break free from this phenomenon is to challenge your fears. Once you challenge your fears, you consider a possibility to win. That's a positive change. Holding onto positive beliefs will distract your mind from negativity and push your mind to a better perspective.

Fear is a possibility,

Possibility is not a fact.

Thoughts are like clouds,

Some are white, some are black.

White thoughts make you dream,

Black thoughts make your day darker.

Pour the negativity down like rain,

Make your day lighter and brighter.

# Blooming Petals

Overthinking repeats like hell loop

But there's always a loophole.

When you scream out your frustrations in an empty cave, your frustrating words come back to you as an echo. Bad thoughts are the same. The more we try to avoid intrusive thoughts, the more it comes back to haunt us like an echo.

This is why analyze your thoughts instead of avoiding them.

Find distraction instead of opposition.

Blooming Petals

Don't let the fear of rejection stop you from trying,

Scentless flowers bloom the prettiest.

If you have the capacity to fight storm for others,

You have the capacity to build a shelter for yourself.

# Blooming Petals

Low self-esteem is like a broken mirror,

No matter how beautiful

Or creative you are,

You will still appear broken.

Jokes that ruin your self-esteem are not jokes,

That's *emotional abuse.*

# Blooming Petals

People who truly care for you don't break you,

They mend you.

Hate is contagious,

It spreads rapidly.

Love is the remedy.

# Blooming Petals

A negative perspective makes you doubt,

A positive perspective makes you proud.

Someone who loves you

Won't gift you a wounded heart

And a scarred self-esteem.

Someone who loves you

Won't repeat to hurt you

Over and over

Again and again.

Observe the repetitive patterns.

Break free.

# Blooming Petals

What hurts you hurts you,

No one will take a share of your pain.

Don't let them draw your boundaries for you.

I hope you allow yourself

To be treated with kindness,

I hope you embrace self-love.

Cut negativity,

Create space for creativity.

It's beautiful how withered leaf falls

So that new leaf can come into life.

Falling apart gives us an opportunity

To be resurrected again.

# Blooming Petals

Believe in hope,

Hope will believe in you.

Believe in happiness,

Happiness will believe in you.

You attract what you vibrate.

People are like currents,

They are always in motion.

They are strong enough to

Cut through the rocks

And deep enough to

Maintain the flow of life.

Blooming Petals

Healing delays when you're in denial,

Be honest with your emotions.

Allow yourself to break

And feel the hurt.

*~Waves break to recreate*

Plant the seed of self-love

Anwesha Das

Self-love blooms the moment

You stop chasing people

And look for love

Within yourself.

Do not make another person your source of happiness. People can change anytime. When they change, you'll be left with nothing but emptiness.

You're the only source of your happiness. Chasing people will never make you feel complete. Only you can complete yourself. The love you're looking for in someone else already exists within you. The nectar of self love is honey sweet.

Why would you chase a butterfly when you're already a honey bee?

Anwesha Das

There's a map inside you.

Discover parts of yourself

That are unknown to you.

Explore yourself,

Know yourself,

Love yourself.

The mistake you often make is that you try to find yourself through the eyes of someone else while you choose to remain a stranger to yourself. When you chase the wrong people in the hope of finding yourself, you end up losing yourself.

You'll never know who is right or who is wrong for you unless *you know yourself.*

Anwesha Das

Self awareness begins with introspection.

Disappointments cloud your judgment when you cannot love yourself.

When you don't love yourself, you attract people into your life who *don't love you either.* That's how the circle of heartbreak never ends.

Invest some time into yourself so you can know all parts of you and fall in love with all parts of you.

Anwesha Das

Self-love is the most wonderful journey of your life.

When the moon gets insecure,

It hides behind the clouds.

When you get insecure,

You hide behind validation.

*~ self validate*

Anwesha Das

Confidence shines brighter than perfection.

Accept all your scars

And all your flawed parts—

The moon shines the brightest

When it stops hiding behind the clouds.

Anwesha Das

When you're drowning in insecurities,

Self-love saves you like a lifeboat.

Body needs oxygen,

Soul needs peace,

Heart needs self-love.

Anwesha Das

There is a thin line between *selfish and self awakening*.

You're self awakening when you take a deeper look within yourself to explore all parts of yourself.

 You self-love when you accept yourself for who you truly are.

There is a wood inside you,

The depths of you are green,

Peace exists within yourself.

*~ inner peace*

When craze turns into sanity,

That's when the soul finds serenity.

Anwesha Das

Inner peace blooms in solitude.

Why do you chase a mirage when there is an oasis inside you?

*~ illusion and truth*

Anwesha Das

Why are you searching for eternity

In someone else when you have a temporary life?

No wonder why you face so many *disappointments*.

Petals fall,

Seasons change,

Reasons change,

People change.

Eternity is now.

Live a happy life

While you're alive.

Anwesha Das

Discover your weakness through breaking,

Test your patience through healing,

Explore your strength through self-loving

The road of the truth starts with yourself,

The road of the deception begins

When you're in denial with yourself.

Anwesha Das

Self-love is the nutrition of the soul.

When you plant the seed of self-love,

You bloom with the loveliest petals.

Bloom like the flowers

Butterflies come and go

But flowers keep on blooming.

People come and go

But an introspective mind keeps

Focusing on self growth.

Anwesha Das

Growth takes time,

Time teaches us patience,

Patience teaches us strength,

Strength makes us evolve.

A confident mind does not seek validation,

A confident mind expands like petals.

Anwesha Das

Not all flowers have a gardener,

Not all people have a lover.

We all have a different meaning in life,

Seek the truth of your life.

Relationship is not the ultimate goal of your life. There is nothing sad or lonely in being single. What's sad and lonely is choosing the wrong partner. What's sad and lonely is being unable to love ourselves. Not everyone has a romantic relationship in their life and that's completely okay. We all have different purposes to serve in life. Seek your purpose. Being different does not categorize you as wrong. It makes you unique. Embrace your uniqueness.

Falling in love with someone  is beautiful but what's more beautiful is *falling in love with yourself.*

Stop begging to them to choose you,

Watch them lose you.

*~ flowers bloom for themselves, not for the butterflies*

You remind me of the wildflowers,

Powerful and beautiful.

*~ keep blooming*

Anwesha Das

There will be love,

There will be hatred.

There will be sunshine,

There will be storm—

The buds will still transform.


~ *Wait for your time to transform*

Wasting your efforts on someone

So they make you a priority is like

Watering the weeds in your garden

Instead of the flowers.

*~ Prioritize yourself*

Anwesha Das

**It will not be easy.** When you have believed for too long that you don't deserve love, when you have allowed people for too long to mistreat you, when you have built a castle of insecurities in your head, it will take a lot of time to break those bricks of self doubts.

It will be difficult and it's time consuming. You have to reflect on all the good qualities in yourself and in the beginning it might be hard to list your good qualities but as you patiently continue introspection, you will discover amazing parts of yourself that you were unaware of before. Slowly, beautifully you will find the treasure within yourself that you've searched for in someone else.

You'll get over the idea that love is fake

When you start loving yourself.

Anwesha Das

The emptiness they left in your heart

Can only be filled with self-love.

Losing someone who hurt your heart

Is actually a big gain.

Gain of a chance to heal yourself,

Gain of a chance to boost self-esteem,

Gain of a chance to introspect,

Gain of a chance to grow and

A chance to love yourself.

Anwesha Das

A positive perspective is a hope that saves you when everything seems to be falling apart.

You are glowing brighter ever since you chose

Self-love over fake love.

Anwesha Das

Your soul wears the color of happiness,

You bloom yellow like a sunflower bud.


~ *you're beautiful*

# Blooming Petals

Your heart has been blooming like a red tulip ever since you got rid of the blues in your heart.

Anwesha Das

Self love is dressing up for yourself

Buying yourself flowers

Taking a walk by the beach

**Alone**

And not feeling lonely about it.

Self-love is being comfortable

At your own company.

# Blooming Petals

Even though your petals fall off every winter

It's beautiful to watch your courage

To keep on blooming every spring,

Even though your heart is cold in winter

It's beautiful to see you dance

In the summer breeze.

Anwesha Das

You sway with breeze

Like a flower on a summer day,

You treat yourself with warmth

Like the petals on a sunny day.

Choosing yourself is not selfish,

Choosing yourself instead of

Waiting for someone to choose you

Is powerful.

Anwesha Das

I shall meet you where the flowers bloom,

At the end of all gloom.

All the places you wandered to search for love

Led you back to yourself—

Finally you found yourself.